This book is affectionately dedicated to the knuckleheads in Grade 6 of SBS in Holmdel, the future Class of 2025. And Mrs. McCahill who invited me to teach them.

# Teacher Appreciation Day

By Lorie Curley

## Chapter 1

Ms. Frogge woke early to put the kettle on. She liked her tea lukewarm and green. Actually, some days, she only took one sip. On those days, she wondered if she preferred making tea to drinking tea. She kept a running list: "Things to Think About".

On this particular morning, she was on time and ready to go. She hopped in her car, a lime green convertible Mini Cooper, and backed out of her driveway. It was 6:25 and still pretty dark.

This is why she did not clearly see the mama goose with her baby geese in the road until it was too late. None of them were injured, but Ms. Frogge had

frightened them into the air and their
mother was furiously squawking.

"Gee whiz!" said Ms. Frogge as she pulled
up to the stop sign. "Can't you find
another place to cross the road?"

Then she chuckled to herself as she tried
to answer the age old riddle,
"Why did the chicken cross the road?"

"Maybe it was going to comfort the
traumatized goose."

## Chapter 2

"Ms. Frogge is nice. She won't care that you forgot your homework," said Dylan. He was waiting for the bus and talking to his sister.

"There she goes!" said A.J. as he spotted Ms. Frogge's lime green car in the distance.

"She yelled at me yesterday," said Sophia. "I think she hates me."

"No way," said Theodora," Ms. Frogge loves everyone, even the annoying boys."

## Chapter 3

Mr. Kupcake took off his reading glasses and stared at his wife over the breakfast table.

"Do you like it?" asked Mrs. Kupcake.

She was referring to the book she had given him to read, " The Nuts and Bolts of Birdwatching".

"The chapters are short. I like that," Mr. Kupcake did not like reading very much. "I like the pictures, too".

"The pictures are beautiful," said Mrs. Kupcake. She was very enthusiastic about birds. She hoped Mr. Kupcake would soon retire from his job as principal at SB Elementary School and join her birdwatching group.

## Chapter 4

Dylan, A.J., Kaitlin, Michael, Kate, Sloane, Cece, Luke, Ava, Colin, and a few other sixth graders who will remain nameless filed into classroom 102. There they sat waiting for Ms. Frogge.

It was 7:35.


## Chapter 5

Where was she?

## Chapter 6

Mr. Kupcake arrived in his office at St. Bartholomew's Elementary School at precisely 7:37. His secretary was making the morning announcements when Dylan came running down the hallway.

"Mr. Kupcake! Mr. Kupcake!" he was yelling.

Mr. Kupcake stepped into the hallway, "Dylan, what is the matter? Why are you yelling and running in the hallway?"

"Mr. Kupcake, Ava hit Francesco. with a ruler and Ella is bouncing the globe."

"Well, where's Ms. Frogge?"

"We don't know. She's not in our room."

Armed with that alarming news, Mr. Kupcake went running and yelling down the hallway toward classroom 102 with Dylan jogging closely behind.

## Chapter 6.5

Mr. Kupcake stood in the doorway and cleared his throat. But no one noticed him. Paper airplanes, and accusations filled the air.

Dylan, who had run to the other door, began waving, pointing and gesticulating madly. The class noticed *him* and quieted down.

"Students!" said Mr. Kupcake. "Take out your Math books. I will be Ms. Frogge until she arrives."

"You don't look like Ms. Frogge," said Grace. Maggie giggled. Mateo began drawing pictures of Mr. Kupcake with a wig. Grace giggled.

"Shush!" thundered Mr. Kupcake.

"What page?" asked Elizabeth, trembling.

"I need to go to band practice," said Joyce..

## Chapter 7

"What's a fraction, again?" asked Alex.

Mr. Kupcake was frazzled. He reached for his phone. "Where is that Frogge!?" he said to himself. "She is always so prompt and reliable…".

"Mr. Kupcake, have you heard from Ms. Frogge, yet?" asked Tyler. He was a very quiet student. He sounded worried.

"Is she sick?" asked Sam.

"Should we worry?" asked Rylee.

"Should we call the police!" asked Leila.

"Should we search the grounds?" asked Lauren.

Then the loudspeaker came on:

"Mr. Kupcake, Mr. Kupcake. Please call the office."

"Is it about Ms. Frogge?" asked Miriam.

"Did they find her body?" asked Charley.


Mr. Kupcake shushed the class as best he could, then stepped into the hallway to call Mrs. Stuffy, the office secretary.

## Chapter 8

"Where is she?" asked Mr. Kupcake. "This is the longest hour of my life! I know nothing about fractions. What have you heard? Is she on her way? Did her car break down? Does she need a ride?"

Mrs. Stuffy couldn't decide which question to answer first. "No," she said. "No, she doesn't need a ride. No, her car didn't break down. And, no she's not on her way."

"Where is she?!" Mr. Kupcake was exasperated.

"We don't know. We called her but there's no answer."

## Chapter 9

"Who is her emergency contact? Did you call her emergency contact?"

"Mr. Kupcake, Faye hit Andrew with a stapler. Can Andrew, Alex and I go to the nurse?" Dylan asked.

Mr. Kupcake scoured at Dylan. Before Dylan could further explain, a stapler went flying over Dylan's head, and past Mr. Kupcake's nose.

Then Robert stepped into the hallway holding a bloody tissue to his forehead. "Can I go to the nurse?"
he asked. Blood dripped onto the floor.

"Call her emergency contact!" snapped Mr. Kupcake.

"Me?" asked Dylan.

"I don't know my emergency contact", said Robert.

"What's an emergennynonact?" asked Sophia.

**PART TWO**

Right about now you may expect the author to begin telling you where Ms. Frogge is...

So, let's find out.

The last time anyone saw her, Ms. Frogge was driving her lime green convertible past the bus stop. A.J.saw her drive by.

What happened next? Here's a chance for you to write your part of the story. Tell me - where do you think Ms. Frogge went? What happened to her? Was it something wonderful? Or something awful? You decide. You write it. Get your own paper. You will need more room than this:

**Author's Version Part Two**

**Chapter 1**

As Ms. Frogge sped along Route 25, she did not notice the giant hole in the road. In fact, she had never seen the giant hole before; it was never ever there before. It just suddenly appeared, like magic.

And, speeding as she was, she had no way to avoid it. In she went! And down, down, down,down, down, well you get the idea...down she went. But to her it felt more like "through". She wasn't dizzy, and she was not thrown from her car.

## Chapter 2

When Ms. Frogge's car finally came to a stop, it was 11:00 am. She had missed homeroom, Math, and ELA.

"Wow!" she thought, "I better call Mr. Kupcake. He will be so worried."

As she dug through her bag looking for her phone, she heard a Tonya Sunshine song playing. She looked up and saw a stage.

"Wow!" she thought, "I think that's Tonya Sunshine.".

She stopped looking for her phone, pulled her bag over her shoulder and walked toward the stage.

## Chapter 3

Tonya sang all Ms. Frogge's favorites. There was a nice crowd and free snacks. Ms. Frogge was enjoying herself so much, she forgot it was a school day.

She was horrified when she looked at her phone. It was 12:20!

Mr. Kupcake had called 48 times. His secretary, Mrs. Stuffy, had left 32 voicemails. Ms. Frogge quickly dialed the school's main number. She had no idea what she should say.

## Chapter 4

The hole in the road was not her fault, but attending a concert? In the middle of the day? On a school day? There was no excuse.

Ms. Frogge quickly concocted a few versions of her morning:

A. My car and my cell phone were stolen.
B. I was delirious with yellow fever.
C. My dog ate my cell phone and my car keys.

She decided to use all three.

" Mr. Kupcake?"
" Ms. Frogge!" Mr. Kupcake sounded rather annoyed.

"I am so sorry to call you this late in the day,"

Then her phone died.

**Chapter 8** ( you may wonder what happened to **Chapter**s 5,6,&7 -we will get to those later)

Dylan was running down the hallway again.

"Faye passed out!" he was yelling.
Mrs. Stuffy stepped out of her office to apprehend him.

"What are you yelling about? Where is the sub?" she crossed her arms and stared at him.

She was in no mood for this 15th interruption. Dylan had been running down the hallway and screaming all morning.

"The sub, the sub, the sub told me to get you", he stammered.

"What happened?" Mrs. Stuffy stomped toward room 102. Dylan skipped beside her trying to explain.

"Faye was opening a window to let a fly out, when Dante spotted a spider. He ..."

"I thought you said Faye passed out?"

"She did. When Dante smashed the spider on his notebook..."

Mrs. Stuffy was furious by the time she reached the classroom.
"Do we need an ambulance?" she asked the sub.

The sub, Mrs. Puffinwinklestein was an extraordinarily tiny woman with a very sing-songy, but screechy voice. Her voice irritated Mrs. Stuffy to tears.

"Gee whiz, I hope not," she screeched.

Faye lay on the floor while Dante and Caitlin knelt beside her. Cecelia stood above her dropping water on her forehead.

Mrs. Stuffy shouted at them, "Back up!"

Her voice was so scary and so loud it made Faye jump. She stood up so quickly she bumped her head on Dante's elbow.

Dante fell to the floor writhing in pain, grabbing his elbow, and sobbing. Faye grabbed her head and stumbled around the room shouting, "Cussion !I have a cussion!"

Tyler got up from his desk and walked like a dinosaur for no reason. Grace giggled. Juliette giggled. Maggie giggled. Kate, CeCe and Lauren rolled out of their desks.

Mrs. Puffinwinklestein ran to the intercom to call for back-up.

Dylan took a moment to correct Faye, "It's 'concussion', stupid, not 'cussion' ".

Mrs. Puffinwinklestein wanted to scold Dylan but she was too preoccupied. She screeched into the intercom "Mr. Kupcake, Mr. Kupcake! Come Quickly! It's a cussion!"

The screeching was too much for Mrs. Stuffy. She covered her ears and staggered into the hallway.

Unfortunately, Mrs. Ohno the school nurse, whom everyone called Mrs. O, was (at that very moment) stepping toward the door that Mrs. Stuffy was staggering out.

Mrs. O was a strong, tall woman, sort of corpulent ( you may need to look that word up) and when Mrs. Stuffy, who was mostly skin and bones ran into her, it was as if Mrs. Stuffy had hit a wall.

Mrs. Stuffy fell to the floor.

Dylan, having run to the door of the classroom, saw the collision and began yelling "Ms. O! Oh! Oh no!"

The class thought this was hilarious. Everyone, including Faye burst into laughter. Chase and Matthew rolled on the floor in tears.

By this time, Mr. Tipinspill, the school's maintenance supervisor who was making his rounds with his giant mop, saw the commotion and began running toward them.

However, and very unfortunately, he did not notice that Ms. Paintit, the art teacher, who they sometimes but not all the time, called Ms. P, was stepping into the hallway to see what all the noise was about. Naturally, he, Mr. Tipinspill, slammed into the door.

Mr. Tipinspill was okay, but Ms.P slipped, and lay with one foot in the doorway, the other unneatly tucked under her bottom. ( If you want to draw a picture of Ms. P on the floor, try to make her look like a pretzel. Her leg was that messed up.)

To recap, Faye was stumbling about grabbing her head; Dante was writhing on the floor holding his elbow, Matthew and Chase were laughing hysterically and rolling about on the floor; Mrs. Stuffy was flat on her back in the hallway, the art teacher, Mrs. P, was halfway in the hall and halfway in her classroom in the shape of a pretzel.

Mrs. O, the nurse, and Mr. Tipinspill, the maintenance man, were standing and staring in disbelief.

It may help if you drew a quick diagram of it here. Or again, get your own paper, since you may make a mistake or want to lend this book to a good friend who may want to draw their own diagram:

Meanwhile ...

**Chapter 9**

Ms. Frogge redialed and redialed and redialed but could not get through.

She tried texting him.

"Mr. Kupcake. I don't know what went wrong. My dog ate my cell phone this morning and the keys to my car."

She decided to hit send before her story got too involved. A long minute went by, then "undelivered ".

She hit send again. "Undelivered".

"Uggh," she looked up in despair. Then someone handed her a large iced coffee with whipped cream.

"Am I dreaming?" she wondered. She took a sip. There was a light hint of caramel. Just the way she liked it.

She turned to thank the person who had given it to her, but she had disappeared.

She looked around and tried to understand where she was. "This is not my town," she thought to herself.

"It's also not any town I have ever seen before,".

She sat on a bench under an enormous oak tree. Opposite her was a walking path. On the other side of the path was a small shop.

She was not certain if the coffee had come from the shop because the sign on the door was hidden by a striped awning that stretched from one side of the building to the other.

Above the awning were windows adorned with flower boxes. And above the windows were more striped awnings.

( Actually, it looked a like a gingerbread house, or a dollhouse, or a little cottage one might find in a fairy tale. It was so perfect it was kind of spooky. If you think you can draw it, please do. Again, please use your own paper because there is not enough room here, especially if you make a mistake and want to redraw it.)

Ms. Frogge was intrigued. She got up from her bench and sauntered across the path into the shop while continuing to sip her perfectly prepared delightfully refreshing iced coffee.

## Chapter 10

Inside the shop were more surprises. Ms. Frogge was surrounded by clothing and accessories and shoes - all in her favorite color, lime green!

"This is nuts!" she declared.

"I am sorry," came a voice from behind the counter, "We don't have nuts."

The voice belonged to a very tall, very thin man dressed in orange from head to toe. His hat was orange, his glasses were orange, shirt, belt, pants, socks, shoes, and shoelaces.

He stood out quite obviously against all
the lime green.

"Oh, I didn't mean I want nuts," Ms.
Frogge tries to explain, "I am having a very
nutty day."

"People are confused by our name," said
the man as he pointed to a sign.
"Pistachios is my name, this is my store,
but we haven't any nuts."

"That's very nutty," Ms. Frogge laughed.

Mr. Pistachio was not as amused.
"Can I help you with something in
particular?" he asked in a snippy voice.

"It may seem strange, but can you tell me where I am? I mean what town are we in?"

"Town?"

"I am kind of lost," said Ms. Frogge.

"This is Nutville. We are in Nutville." Mr. Pistachio said. "Would you like to buy a map?"

"Nutville?" Ms. Frogge wanted to laugh again, but she thought better of it. " May I look at a map? I never heard of Nutville before.. I am very confused... I was ..."

Mr. Pistachio held up his hand to quiet Ms. Frogge, he raised his phone to his ear.

"Yes," he said into the phone.

"Yes," he said again.

"Okay", he said and then clicked off, and returned to Ms. Frogge.

"What were you saying?"

"I was asking for a ..."

"Excuse me," yet again Mr. Pistachio answered his phone. This time Ms. Frogge wandered to the shelves in the back of the store where Mr. Pistachio stashed the books, "and maybe a map", she hoped.

"I really have to get out of here," she said to herself. She noticed a door in the back of the store and, also an elevator.

"Nuts and Bolts, Jokes and Riddles, Lime and Lemon," Ms. Frogge read the titles of the books out loud.

"Weird," she said, also out loud.

"What's weird?" Mr. Pistachio was standing beside her.

"Oh, sorry, I was talking to myself, is there a map in one of these books?" she asked again.

Meanwhile…

## Chapter 11

"Darn, darn, darn!" Mr. Kupcake was shouting at his phone again.

It was 1:30. Although the school day was almost over, Mr. Kupcake desperately needed to know-and understand- what happened to Ms. Frogge?

**Chapters 5, 6 and 7**
( as promised earlier)

"Please sit, sit down, please," said Mrs. Puffinwinklestein, the sub, as she entered Room 102.

Her very screechy voice quickly quieted the quibbling children of 6th grade.

But trouble was brewing:
From behind their desks, out of Mrs. Puffinwinklestein's view, A.J. and Grady squeezed glue all over their hands. And giggled. Mrs. Puffinwinklestein stared at them.

They stopped giggling, sat up straight and tall, and waited innocently for their chance to attack.

When Mrs. Puffinwinklestein turned her back to write on the board, the boys leapt from their desks and slapped their gluey hands on Ronald's back.

"No!" screamed Ronald.

Turning, Mrs. Puffinwinklestein pointed at Ronald screeching, "You! Detention!"

By the end of the ELA session, Ronald, Colin, Alex, Luke, Michael, Marco and Faye had been attacked by A.J. and Grady's gluey hands. And - they had all been sentenced to detention.

By the time recess rolled around, another three children were put in detention. Jamie, Andrew, and Donavan.

Somehow A.J. and Grady had escaped Mrs. Puffinwinklestein's ire and eye.

But revenge was coming!

## Chapter 5.5

After lunch, Jamie, Andrew, Donavan, Ronald,  Luke, Cece, Sloan, Michael, Marco and Kate gathered on the detention bench and made a plan.

"Let's tie their shoes together," suggested Sloan.

"That's not mean enough," said Cece.

"Let's draw permanent marker mustaches on their faces!" said Kate.

"That's more like it," said Cece.

Ronald laughed.

"Let's put their textbooks in the toilet," said Jamie.

"Let's tell Mr. Kupcake that A.J. and Grady are holding Mrs.Frogge in a cage in their basement", said Michael.

As luck would have it, just as Michael said "cage in basement' Mrs. Stuffy was walking in the hallway. She overheard the part about Grady and AJ and Ms. Frogge in the cage in but not the "Let's tell them" part.

Mrs. Stuffy did not understand that Michael was merely suggesting that someone should tell someone in authority that Grady and AJ were holding ...

Well, you understand – right?

ANYHOW...and furthermore...

Mrs. Stuffy ran into Mr. Kupcake's office and repeated what she heard:

"Mr. Kupcake, A.J. and Grady are holding Mrs. Frogge captive in a cage! In their basement!"

## Chapter 6

You can imagine what happened next.
Poor Mr. Kupcake was beside himself.

"What shall I do?" he screamed.
"What's to be done?!"

"You need to rescue her - of course," said
Mrs. Stuffy. "You must! You have no other
choice. We cannot last another day here
at SB Elementary. We need Ms. Frogge!"

Mr. Kupcake knew she was right. He
grabbed his car keys and raced to the door
where he yelled, "Text me the address!"

Mrs. Stuffy frantically copied and pasted
the addresses of AJ and Grady and sent
them to Mr. Kupcake's cell phone.

They pinged on his phone just as he started his engine. He looked at them and realized they were in two completely different directions. AJ lived to the east, and Grady lived to the west.

"Darn!" said Mr. Kupcake. "I will have to make a guess." Then he stared, "Eenie meenie minnie, mo.."

AJ's house won. Mr. Kupcake headed east on Route 25. But as he neared the stop sign, he saw a giant hole, or maybe it was a tunnel? He tried to slam on his brakes, but his car went straight into the pitch dark hole.

Down, down, down he went, ( or maybe it was through). He wasn't sure. All he knew was he was still in his car when it finally stopped.  He looked around and saw a bench under a giant oak tree.

## Chapter 12  ( Or 7?)

Is it possible? What do you think? Will Mr. Kupcake find Ms. Frogge? Will they find them? Is this just a dream? Are you asleep?

You can write your ideas here:

Or, keep reading... after all, you paid for this book. You may as well get your money's worth.

## Chapter 13

( The bad luck chapter)

Mrs. Stuffy went out to the recess yard to ask AJ and Grady about the cage in their basement.

AK was shooting hoops. Grady was covering him. Mrs. Stuffy ran on to the court and blew her whistle. AJ ignored her, took the shot, but missed.

"Airball!" Danny shouted.

The ball ricocheted off the rim and hit Chase square on the nose. Blood gushed. Everyone screamed.

Mrs. Stuffy blew her whistle again. Again, no one paid any attention. Grady took off his white fleece jacket and offered it to Chase.

Chase took the jacket and wiped his nose. The fleece turned red. Again, everyone screamed.

This time Mrs. Stuffy used her phone to call the nurse.

"Mrs. O,"she shouted.

"What is it now?"asked Mrs. O ( she was quite exhausted by the day of subs and accidents).

"We need you in the .." but before she could finish her sentence, a baseball thrown from the field by an extremely talented pitcher from the 8th grade varsity team, knocked her to the ground.

"Uh oh", said AJ.

"Yikes," said the very talented pitcher from the 8th grade varsity, John Vincent.

AJ picked up her phone.

"Mrs. O? Are you still there?"

"What's going on?" Mrs. O sounded very annoyed.

"Can you please come to the recess yard? We have a situation. Well, two situations. Actually."

## Chapter 13.5

Mrs. O looked around her office. Faye was laying on a cot with an ice bag on her head. She was waiting for her grandmother to pick her up.

Dante was sitting on a chair holding a bag of ice to his elbow. He was waiting for his father to pick him up.

Ms. Paintit, the art teacher, was sitting with her leg resting on top of a desk. She too had a bag of ice.

"I'll be right back," she said to the group. "please don't follow me."

Mrs. O stomped down the hallway through the double doors to the recess yard. Faye got up and followed her quietly. She needed to see what was going on.

Immediately, she spotted the chaos. Mrs. Stuffy lay on the basketball court surrounded by a group of Ms. Frogge's 6th graders. Beside Mrs. Stuffy , Chase sat holding a bloody jacket to his nose.

"Mrs. O!" yelled AJ. "Make way!" The crowd parted allowing Mrs. O a better view of Mrs. Stuffy.

Her eyes were shut. Her hair which was sort of a mess on a good day was extremely discombobulated. Some of it covered her cheek, some was in her mouth, the rest seemed stuck to the pavement.

"Is she alive?" asked Danny,

"It was John who threw it. Johnny the Rebels starting pitcher," offered Sam. He pointed to the field.

Mrs. O took Mrs. Stuffy's hand in her own and felt for a pulse.

## Chapter 14

Mr. Kupcake got out of his car.
"Where the heck am I?"

Siri tried to answer him.

"You are in a town called Nutville" it told
him.

"Nutville? That makes sense," said Mr.
Kupcake. He knew it was a funny
comment, but he was not feeling any
humor at all. He just wanted this terrible
day to end; and he wanted Ms. Frogge
back to school.

"It does not make sense to Siri," said Siri.

Mr. Kupcake ignored her. He walked toward the bench under the oak tree. From there he saw something lime green in a ditch.

"Could it be?" he wondered. "Could Ms. Frogge also be here -unnexpectedly- in Nutville?".

Siri answered, "Maybe".

He walked toward the car to look at the plates. Sure enough they read "FGY 22" .

"That's her car!" he cheered out loud. "I made a wrong turn, but this may be right!"

**Chapter 15**

Ms. Frogge was busy staring at the map when a doorbell rang. Mr. Pistachio excused himself.

He hurried to the front door. He peered out and saw Mr. Kupcake leaning against the door with his hands cupped over his eyes, trying to see inside. Mr. Pistachio pressed an intercom and spoke into it.

"Only one customer at a time, sir. You'll have to wait."

"I'm looking for someone," he stammered back. "Is there a woman there? Is Ms. Frogge there? Can you tell me? It's important that I find her."

But the intercom was old and rusty.
Mr. Pistachio only heard "Rrrrr, uhhhh
ffff".

"What?" he asked.

Mr. Kupcake only heard "Pha?"

Ms. Frogge scooted to the door,shoved
Mr. Pistachio out of the way, and pulled it
open.

"Mr. Kupcake!" she exclaimed.

## Chapter 16

"What are you doing here? Actually, what am I doing here? Actually, where are we?" asked Ms. Frogge all in one breath.

"Good question!" said Mr. Pistachio in his most annoyed tone yet. "I need you both out of here! Now!" he shouted, then whistled. In an instant three dark brown shorthaired ( very cute) dachshunds came racing and barking and biting from the back of the shop.

"Get em"!" yelled Mr. Pistachio.

Mr. Kupcake and Ms. Frogge flew out the door, running as fast as they could to the safety of the bench where they jumped to a low tree branch and hung with the dogs barking below. Mr. Pistachio whistled again and the dogs returned to him.

"And don't come back!" he said as he slammed the shop door.

"Where are we?" said Mr. Kupcake as he dangled from the branch.

"In an oak tree," said Siri.

"I think we are going to need to get back in that shop, Mr. Kupcake. I think the answer to our questions is in there somewhere."

"He didn't seem to like us much,"

"No, but we can get back. Let's make a plan,"

"We are good at plans - Ms. Frogge, you and I," said Mr. Kupcake.

"Step one," said Ms. Frogge," let's get out of this tree."

She let go of the branch and landed safely on the bench. Mr. Kupcake did the same.

"So what do we do next?" asked Mr. Kupcake.

"Let's review what we know so far," said Ms. Frogge.

"Okay,' said Mr. Kupcake. "We know we are lost…"

"We know we were driving down RT 25, "

"Yes, it was definitely RT 25. I was headed east, were you headed west?"

"I was headed to school, so I guess that was west. Yes, Mr. Kupcake I was headed west. So that means…"

"That means the hole we entered…"

"Or tunnel…"

"Or tunnel, was located in both directions."

"Yes"

"That doesn't help much," said Siri.

"I have to agree with Siri," said Ms. Frogge. "What else do we know?"

"We know we are not dreaming." said Mr. Kupcake.

"How do we know that?" asked Ms. Frogge.

"Well, we know we are lost?" asked Mr. Kupcake.

"This is stupid," said Siri.

"I agree with you," said Ms. Frogge again to Siri. "But we know we are in a place called Nutville. We know got here while traveling on RT 25. So we can rule out the Land of Oz."

"That's true," said Mr. Kupcake," there was no tornado, or Munchkins..."

"Not yet," said Ms. Frogge.

"No flying monkeys..." said Mr. Kupcake.

"I hate flying monkeys," said Ms. Frogge. "Let's hope there are no flying monkeys."

"What about other people - or shops? Have you seen anyone else?"

"When I first got here there was a concert. It was right over there," Ms. Frogge pointed to an open field. "But everyone left. I haven't seen anyone since I wandered into the store. I spent a long time sitting on this bench trying to make a call to you.I am so sorry, Mr. Kupcake. I tried calling all morning."

Ms. Frogge started to cry. Mr. Kupcake tried to console her. But it only made him cry too. They were babbling and crying like babies.

"We miss you dearly, Ms. Frogge. As you can imagine. Grade 6 is a disaster. The sub is no Frogge, Ms. Frogge. When I heard you were being held captive by AJ and Grady I rushed out to save you."

"AJ and Grady?! Captive!? What are you talking about?" Ms. Frogge wiped her eyes and stopped sniffling.

While Mr. Kupcake tries to explain the goings-on at SB Elementary School, let's see what's going on there now...

**Chapter 17**

It was now 1:00 at SB Elementary School.
The bell had rung and recess was over.
The main office was being run by the sub,
Mrs. Puffinwinklestein because Mr.
Kupcake and Mrs. Stuffy were – well –
let's say, unavailable, or preoccupied. (You
can circle which word you prefer.)

Mrs. O, the overworked, very tall, rather
corpulent school nurse, was waiting for
the ambulance to take Mrs. Stuffy, who
was equally overworked, but not as
overweight, in fact, somewhat
underweight, who had been hit by a
baseball thrown at her head
(by accident) by the best pitcher on the 8th
grade varsity, John Vincent, or as his
friends called him – Johnny V.

Ms. Frogge's sixth graders who had been at recess when the commotion began and the sixth graders who had been in detention when the commotion began sat somberly on the curb outside the school under the very diligent watch of the Security guard Mr. Lemmonayd.

"Do you think Ms. Frogge will be in tomorrow?" Dylan asked Mr. Lemmonayd.

"I hope so; we've had way too many casualties today," he said. Then he counted them up. "First, the concussion, then the ...

"elbow..." Matthew added.

"the broken leg ..." added Chase.

"the bloody nose," said Grady.

" then the death? " asked Faye.

"is she dead?" asked Caitlin.

"Not yet," said Mr. Lemmonayd. "Mrs. O says she is in a coma. We have to hope the ambulance shows up – fast!"

"Maybe we should pray," said Matthew.

"That's a good idea," said Mr. Lemmonayde. "We definitely need some help."

The sixth graders who were sitting on the curb all began to pray in unison, 'Hail Mary, full of grace, the Lord is with thee, Blessed are thou among women and blessed is the fruit of thy womb, Jesus. Holy Mary, mother of God, pray for us sinners, now and at the hour of our death."

"Amen" they said together. And silence fell over the group. And they were calm.

## Chapter 18

But they still worried...

"Do you think Johnny V will go to prison?" asked Joey.

"I don't think he hit Mrs. Stuffy on purpose," said Grady.

"He will probably be in prison – but only if she dies," said Dylan.

"They will let him out after a few months," said Grady.

"We can bust him out," said Dylan.

"Here comes the ambulance!" yelled Faye.

"Our prayers are answered," said Mr. Lemmonayde.

The ambulance pulled up to the curb. The sixth graders jumped to their feet. And began cheering. "Let's go Ms. O".

Ms. O, Tyler and Johnny V. carried Mrs. Stuffy to the stretcher. The EMT's quickly strapped her in and hooked her up to an IV pole.

"She'll be okay," Tom the EMT said to the 6th graders. "Don't you worry."

As the ambulance drove away, Mrs. Stuffy sat up in the back and waved. Johnny V. sighed a sigh of relief.

"Good news," Joey said to Johnny, "it looks like you are not going to prison after all."

"Not yet!" said Mr. Lemmonayde. Johnny. Joey, Tyler and Mrs. O laughed.

The 6<sup>th</sup> graders stopped chanting and walked back into the school. It had been quite a day. But it was only 1:30. Time for Art class.

**Chapter 19**

Ms. Paintit was on her way to the hospital for x-rays of her leg. Mrs. Puffinwinklestein was working in the office to cover for Mrs. Stuffy, so Mr. Lemmonayde offered to teach the Art class.

The sixth graders greeted him with shouts and chants. ( The sixth grade loved to chant.) They formed a long line and began swaying with their arms around each other:

"Lemon – ayde, Lemon-ayde, Lemon-ayd," they chanted in unison.

They chanted so loudly, that they could not hear the announcement over the loud speaker. Mrs. Puffinwinklestein was warning the school to lock down.

Victor, a Siberian Husky, was lose in the school. Mrs. Puffinwinklestein was screeching into the intercom, "Victor is loose. Please shelter in place. Code Yellow."

Victor was running joyfully down the empty hallways when he heard the chanting. He loved chanting. He also loved Chase and Juliette and Andrew. He could smell them from the hallway.

As Mrs. Puffinwinklestein made her screechy announcement for the third time, Victor came racing into the Art room.

He ran straight at the chorus line. The chanting stopped, and the class erupted in giggles. Then a new chant started, "Victor! Victor, Victor!"

Mr. Lemonayde who was terrified of Victor jumped onto the desk, and shouted "Stop!"

His voice was so loud, the entire class went quiet, even Victor stopped. He sat in the middle of the room panting.

"I will take him to the office," said Chase. "Can I go with him?" asked Dante and Juliette.

"Yes, please do!" said Mr. Lemonayde.

"Why are you so frightened?" asked Michael.

"Yeah," said Kate, "Victor is the nicest puppy in all the world.

"Let me tell you a story," said Mr. Lemonnayde. The class loved stories, especially the ones Mr. Lemonnayde told. They all sat down in their seats and quietly listened.

"One time when I was 5 years old, I was invited to a birthday party. It was summer time. We were all outside at this kid's house; I think his name was Kurt. Kurt had a really nice backyard.

He had trees, and a tree fort, and lots of grass. For his birthday party he also had a tent. We were having a game of war. Some of us were in the tent and some of us were in the tree fort. I was in the tent.

The tent was about this big." Mr. Lemonnayde pointed to the carpet on the floor. It was a square shape about 4 feet by 5 feet.

"There were 4 of us in the tent. We were sitting in there. My friend Alison, Kurt who was having the party and Alex were in the tree fort. But we could hear them making a plan. We were sure they were going to attack.

The tent was kind of hot, so I went to the door of the tent to peek at the tree fort, and let some cool air into the tent. When out of nowhere this giant animal that looked like a bear came barreling in. Like this, " Mr. Lemmonadye stood up and growled at the 6th graders.

They laughed and laughed.

## Chapter 20

"Time to draw!" said Mr. Lemmonayde. He passed out paper and crayons and colored pencils.

"Can I draw the dog that scared you?" asked Juliette.

"Can I draw Johhny V. hitting Mrs. Stuffy with a baseball?" asked Joey.

"Can I draw Mr. Tipinspill knocking over Ms. Paintit?" asked Ella.

"Yes, yes and yes," said Mr. Lemmonayde. 'Draw whatever you like. The day is almost over."

"Can I make a get well card for Mrs. Stuffy?" asked AJ.

"Yes that's a great idea," said Mr. Lemmonayde.

You can draw whatever you want, also. But get your own paper, please. I need this space to tell you what is happening to Ms. Frogge and Mr. Kupcayke – remember them?

They are in that strange town, Nutville. When we last read about them they were in an oak tree. Remember? Mr.Pistachio had tossed them out of his very weird store and then sent his dogs to chase them.

Do you remember what kind of dogs they were? If you know what they look like, draw them. Also, you can give them names. I haven't named them yet.

Let's see if they have come up with a plan yet..

## Chapter 21

"I thought I saw a back door when I was looking for a map," said Ms. Frogge.

She and Mr. Kupcake were still sitting on the bench. But Ms. Frogge had retrieved a notebook and pen from her bottomless bag of supplies. Mr. Kupcake was staring at his phone. He seemed worried.

"It's almost 2:00," he said. "Everyone will be so worried about us. But I have zero bars on my phone."

"How do you think I feel? I have been stuck here all day. It started out okay, but I really want to get back to school too. I love those 6$^{th}$ graders." Mrs. Frogge began to cry.

Mr. Kupcake offered her a tissue from his pocket. She wiped her eyes, then blew her nose really, loudly.

It was so loud, that the noise knocked Mr. Kupcake off the bench!

This made them both laugh.

"Let's try the backdoor, said Mr. Kupcake as he stood up and wiped some grass off his pants.

"Let's!" said Ms. Frogge. She was feeling optimistic as she crossed the path toward the shop.

They walked around the back and found the door very easily. But before they pulled it open, Ms. Frogge reached into her bottomless bag of supplies to find 6 milkbones.

"Why?Why do you have those?" Mr. Kupcake asked. He was very surprised that a teacher like Ms. Frogge would own a dog. She spent so much time at school, he could not imagine her having enough time to walk and care for a dog.

"You don't have a dog. Do you?" he asked.

(As they are about to enter the shop, you may wonder why a writer like myself would slow the action down to tell a story about why Ms. Frogge had 6 milkbones in her bottomless bag of supplies. And you would be right to question me – after all, my job as the writer is to deliver an interesting story – a story that holds your attention and keeps you at the edge of your seat. So, you can skip this next page, and come back to it later. But, it's true. Ms. Frogge once owned a very special dog.

Ms. Frogge stopped a moment and looked deeply into Mr. Kupcake's dark green eyes. Then she began to tell him the story of Lucy-lu.

"Two years ago a friend of mine, Minne, was moving into an apartment in a small town in Ohio.

We had been friends in 6<sup>th</sup> grade at SB
Elementary School. Minnie and I played
basketball together. We spent all our
spare time together — recess, lunch,
weekends. We were the best of best
friends.

When she packed up to move, I was so so
sad. She said to me, 'Fanny, take my dog,'
"

"Fanny? Ms. Frogge, I didn't know your
friends called you Fanny," said Mr.
Kupcake.

"Yes, it's my nickname. My fullname is
Ferna Fawn Frogge,"

"I did not know that," said Mr. Kupcake, then to get her moving along with his story because he was honestly getting a little impatient, he said, "and the dog?".

"Yes, well, Minnie gave me Lucy-lu. And she and I lived happily together for two years. But, like you said, it was not easy because I do spend a lot of time at school. Lucy had to learn how to make her own lunch."

Obviously, this last comment made Mr. Kupcake wonder – how did Lucy-lu, the dog, learn how to make her own lunch. But, he also realized – "wow, this story is getting way too long."

So. Instead of asking, "How on earth did your dog learn to make it's own lunch?" He simply said:

"Ms. Frogge, maybe we should get going here..." He motioned to the door. And opened it.

## Chapter 22 ( you can skip this chapter if you are in a hurry to get to the end..)

Did you want to know how Ms. Frogge taught her dog Lucy-lu to make her own lunch?

She discovered that Lucy could jump on the kitchen counter, open a cabinet, and knock over the bag of delicious chicken flavored Nibblebits. But she could not spill out one portion. She would spill the entire bag.

Ms. Frogge needed a way for Lucy to pour just the right amount into her bowl.

For a week, Ms. Frogge thought about the problem. She drew many diagrams of Lucy and the kitchen counter and the bowl and the cabinet.

Finally, after many drawings, she came up with this plan:

Every Sunday night Ms. Frogge would bake 5 meatballs stuffed with chicken flavored Nibblebits. Then she would take the meatballs and freeze them in a bowl of water. On Monday morning she would put one of the frozen meatballs into a bowl.

Before she would leave for work, she put Lucy outside in the yard. In the yard, Ms.

Frogge had purchased a small house for Lucy on smallhouses.com. In the house was a fluffy, fleece bed for napping. In the yard, itself, under the bushes and in the surrounding trees were hundreds of chipmunks that needed constant chasing. Lucy loved the backyard and her job as chief-chipmunk chaser.

With the help of the science teacher, Ms. Doit, Ms. Frogge installed a small door with a timer on it that allowed Lucy to enter the house for lunch. Every day at 1:25, the door would open and call Lucy-lu's name.

Above the small door, Ms. Frogge had installed a camera, so she could watch Lucy enter the house to eat her lunch and make sure that none of the chipmunks followed her inside. ( This happened at least once, but this is not the best time to tell that story.)

By 1:25 the frozen meatball stuffed with chicken flavored Nibblebits sat in a puddle of water, just the way Lucy liked it.

So, did Lucy-lu actually learn to make her own lunch? Maybe not. But she was a very self-sufficient little puggle.

## Chapter 22 ( this one is important to the plot)

The back door to the shop opened. And luckily, it did not creak, and it did not knock anything off the shelves. And – no dogs barked.

Mr. Kupcake pointed to what looked like an elevator. Ms. Frogge understood. She stepped toward it and pushed the "up" button.

As the elevator doors separated, they quickly hopped in. They could see Mr. Pistachio was straightening some sweaters in the window. He had his back to them.

"Phew!" said Ms. Frogge as the elevator began to rise. "I don't know where we will end up, but at least Mr. Pistachio didn't see us."

"Let's hope we can find a working phone, a map, and maybe a snack of two up here."

The doors opened to the second floor of the shop. There in the wall was a giant map.

"Hurray!" said Ms. Frogge.

"Look at this," said Mr. Kupcake. He held up a tray of bagels.

"And this!" said Ms. Frogge. She pointed to a phone on a desk.

"It's perfect!" said Mr. Kupcake. "Now where are we?"

The two stared at the map. They could see an X marking the shop; they could see the little path that led to the bench and the oak tree. But where was the school? Where was RT 25?

Mr. Kupcake spread some cream cheese on his bagel. He offered half to Ms. Frogge.

"This map makes no sense," she said as she chomped into the bagel.

"Maybe we should call the school," said Mr. Kupcake in a muffled eating-a-bagel voice. "They can send an Uber to pick us up."

"Good idea, let's call Mrs. Stuffy. She will know how to get us out of here."

Mr. Kupcake began to dial. It was an old rotary phone. It took him several tries to get his fingers into the correct holes, and let it spin back.

Ms. Frogge tried to be patient, but she was feeling very anxious. She was worried that Mr. Pistachio would be on his way up for a snack.

Finally, Mr. Kupcake finished dialing. He heard the ringing. He held the receiver out so that Ms. Frogge could also hear:

"Ring,"

"Ring"

"Ring"

## Chapter 23

Mrs. Puffinwinklestein heard the phone ringing but she tripped and fell on Mrs. Stuffy's wheeled, spinning chair. The chair scooted across the office with Mrs. Puffinwinklestein sprawled face down on top. She let out a very screechy scream.

Fortunately, Michael, who had been sent to the principal's office for talking too much, heard her cry, and the phone. An agile athlete, he held out one hand to stop the chair, and with the other he picked up the phone.

"SB Elementary School, Michael speaking. How may we assist you?" he said.

"Michael? It's Mr. Kupcake. Please, please we need your help. Is Mrs. Stuffy there?"

Michael was confused. He thought Mr. Kupcake was in his office. He thought maybe this person was a fake. He also thought the real Mr. Kupcake would know that Mrs. Stuffy had been hit by a baseball. He looked at Mrs. Puffinwinklestein with a furrowed brow.

Mrs. Puffinwinklestein took the phone from Michael. "Can I help you sir?"

"Who is this?" asked Mr. Kupcake.

"It's Mrs. Puffiniwinklestien" said Mrs. Puffinwinklestein, with her very screechy voice, "I am the sub for Ms. Frogge who has gone missing."

On the other end of the phone, Mr. Kupcake held the phone away from his ears. Her voice was THAT screechy. Ms. Frogge stood beside him motioning for him to hurry up. She was getting more and more anxious. She worried that Mr. Pistachio was about to interrupt them.

"Listen, Mrs. Puffinwinklestein, this is Mr. Kupcake. I am with Ms. Frogge and we are in a town called Nutville. And we are at a shop called Pistachio's. Can you write that down. And can you please send an Uber to pick us up. We need a ride back to the school. Please!"

"Mr. Kupcake, let me get some paper, Hold on," she said.

Mr. Kupcake and Ms. Frogge began to panic. They heard the elevator moving. They stayed on the phone and hid behind the desk.

"Okay, you are at Nutville in Pistachio and you need a ride??" repeated Mrs. Puffinwinklestein.

"We are in Nutville at Pistachio. Pistachio is the name of the shop. We don't know the street address. You will need to look it up for us. Can you do that, Mrs. Puffinwinklestein?" Mr. Kupcake was whispering into the phone. From his hiding place under the desk, he could see the elevator doors opening and Mr. Pisatchio's shoes.

Just as Mrs. Puffinwinklestein said, "Okay", he heard Mr. Pisatchio.

"Fi, fie, fo-fum!" and with that the three menacing dogs came racing around the desk.

## Chapter 24

Mrs. Puffinwinklestein hung up the phone. It was 2:40, time for her to start calling the children to exit the building,

She was flustered and frantic.

"Good grief!" she said.

"What's the matter?" asked Michael. He was happy to help – anything to get himself out of trouble.

"What should I do?" she asked him. "There's so much to do!"

I'll look up the address to the shop," he said, "You call the bus numbers."

Michael sat at Mr. Kupcake's desk and tried to google Pistachio in Nutville. But, of course, he did not know Mr. Kupcake's passwords.

He tried, "Cake1234" and "1234Cake#" but to no avail.

"Darn," he said. Then he had a better idea. He ran down the hallway to the nurse's office. Mrs. O was sitting at her desk.

"What's wrong?" asked Mrs. O.

"Apparently, Mr. Kupcake and Ms. Frogge are in some kind of trouble," he told Mrs. O. "To rescue them I need to look up Pistachio's in Nutville. May I use your computer?"

"That's weird," said Mrs. O.

"Nutville is weird?" asked Michael, "Or Pistachio's?"

"That they are at Pistachio's during the school day," said Mrs. O.

"What is Pistachio's?" asked Michael.

"No, I don't know what it is. Or, where. It's just weird. I thought Ms. Frogge was in Grady's basement in a cage."

Michael was very confused. But then he realized that the rumor he started had been overheard. "Uh oh," he thought. "I better change the subject quickly."

His mischievous mind whirred to deliver:

"Well, can you help me, Mrs. O.? Can you look up what street Pistachio's is on in Nutville? Please."

"Sure" said Mrs. O. "That is a lot easier than treating a concussion, a bruised elbow, a twisted ankle and a coma."

Michael laughed. He stood beside Mrs. O and stared at her screen. He took a pen and a sheet of paper from her desk. They watched the google circle as it spun and spun.

## Chapter 25

Finally, the address appeared.

"Pistachio's Shop
110 Oaktree Street
Nutville"

"That's odd," said Mrs. O, "There's no state."

Michael wrote it down. "Should I take it to Mrs. Puffinwinklestein?" he asked. "Or, should we keep looking?"

"Let me try their webpage," said Mrs. O. She clicked again. An image appeared on the screen of the little shop. She scrolled to the bottom of the page where she expected to find contact information, or directions.

"Ah," she said. She read as she clicked "Directions to our Shop".

## Chapter 26

### Meanwhile in Nutville…

Ms. Frogge had climbed onto the desk. Mr. Kupcake stood on the chair. The dogs yelped but could not reach them.

Mr. Pistachio glared at them from the other side of the room. "Just what are you doing here? I thought I threw you two out!"

Then he whistled to the dogs; they ceased their attack and sat at attention.

"We want to leave," begged Ms. Frogge. "We really do. We just needed to call for a ride."

"We mean you no harm," added Mr. Kupcake. "We don't know where we are, or how we got here. We just want to go back to SB Elementary."

Mr. Pistachio seemed to think this over for a few minutes. He slowly began to grin. And for a split second, Ms. Frogge thought he might just help them out.

"Please, Mr. Pistachio, can you help us?" she begged again.

"What do you want me to do,exactly?"

"You could give us directions back to SB Elementary School," said Mr. Kupcake.

"I have never heard of SB Elementary," said Mr. Pistachio.

Ms. Frogge started to cry. "I have to get back. I don't want to spend the rest of my life in Nutville."

Quite, honestly, she was blubbering. There was all kinds of yick running out of her nose. She could barely talk. Mr. Kupcake searched his pockets for some Kleenex.

Mr. Pistachio also searched his pockets. AS they both found some, the phone on the desk began ringing.

It startled them and made them all jump. Mr. Pistachio leaned across the desk and picked it up.

"Good afternoon, Pistachio's. How may I help you?" he asked in the most pleasant tone he could muster.

"Yes, yes, yes," he said. Then he hung up.

"There's a driver outside waiting for you two," he said.

## Chapter 27

Immediately, Ms. Frogge stopped whimpering. And Mr. Kupcake peered out the window.

"He's right!" said Mr. Kupcake. "I see a car!"

The car, a bright orange Lamborghini, was parked on the other side of the street with its wing-like doors open and its blinkers blinking. A driver dressed entirely in white stood beside the car.

Mr. Pistachio walked to the window too. His dogs followed him and stood on their hind legs to reach the windowsill.

"Wow!" he said. "I love that car." The dogs wagged their tails in agreement.

"Let's get going," Mr. Kupcake whispered to Ms. Frogge.

The two started tiptoed toward the elevator as Mr. Pistachio continued to stare at the car.

"I wonder where that came from," he said to himself.

## Chapter 28

As they climbed into the Lamborghini, which was not easy, Mr. Kupcake asked the driver to share his location and directions with him.

"We will need to come back later for our cars," he explained to Ms. Frogge.

But the driver did not reply. Mr. Kupcake asked again.

But the driver ignored him again.

They were going quite fast. Ms, Frogge grabbed hold of the handle on the door. She felt like she was riding Space Mountain, or KIngda Ka, or El Toro.

Mr. Kupcake asked again. His face was shaking as if her were in a rocket.

Then the car suddenly stopped.

And there they were - at SB Elementary! The doors opened, they got out and the mysterious driver sped off.

It was 3:30.

The school was empty. And quiet.

Ms. Frogge looked in the parking lot and saw her lime green Mini Cooper; Mr. Kupcake's car was parked next to it.

For years and years, this story has been told over, and over again at SB Elementary.

To this day, no one knows how to get to Nutville.

**THE END**

**Questions for the Reader:**

1. What color was Ms. Frogge's car?
2. How many dogs chased her and Mr. Kupcake?
3. What kind of dogs were they?
4. What was Ms. Frogge's friend's name?
5. How was the Uber driver dressed?
6. What prayer did the children pray for Mrs. Stuffy?
7. Why was Mrs. Stuffy in a coma?
8. What was the name of the EMT?
9. What does the word corpulent mean?
10. Which character was the funniest?
11. Which characters were the most helpful?
12, Which characters got hurt?
13. Which chapter was the least important?
14. What hobby did Mr. Kupcake's wife want him to take up?
15. Where is Nutville?

**Disclaimers:**

The characters are fictional; any names that call to mind real people are coincidental and their traits are greatly exaggerated. Tyler, for example, would never get up from his desk and walk like a dinosaur for no reason.

Furthermore, none of the teachers at the real SBS screeched, or panicked, or disappeared. The nurse, maintenance crew and security personnel are very competent and resourceful.

If you have any specific complaints, or questions please direct them to the author at unita.writer@gmail.com.

Made in the USA
Middletown, DE
14 September 2023

38259401R00066